The FRANK PERDUE Way

Simple Steps.
Super Success.

Mitzi Perdue

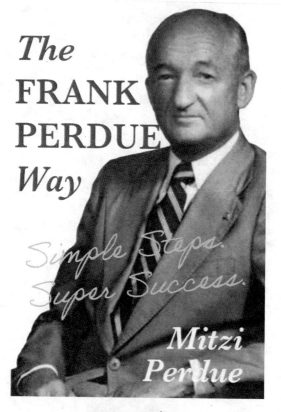

TREMENDOUS
LEADERSHIP
Leadership with a kick!

Life-Changing Classics • Volume XXXIV

The Frank Perdue Way:
Small Steps. Super Success.
Mitzi Perdue

Published by
Tremendous Leadership
PO Box 267
Boiling Springs, PA 17007
717-701-8159 • 800-233-2665

www.TremendousLeadership.com

ISBN-13 978-1-949033-65-6

Printed in the United States of America

CONTENTS

INTRODUCTION

Humble Beginnings

When **Frank Perdue was born in** 1920, his parents Arthur and Pearl had no way to know their only son would end up becoming a household name. Growing up in Salisbury, Maryland, on the Delmarva Peninsula, an area long known for agriculture and trade, Frank started helping around the farm as soon as he could hold an egg in his two little hands. And the rest, as they say, is history.

As an entrepreneur, Frank grew his poultry company from a father-and-son operation to a multi-million dollar corporation that today provides jobs for 20,000 people and, in a good year, sells its products in more than 50 countries.

You may know him as the first CEO to become the spokesperson in his innovative television ads claiming, "It takes a tough man to make a tender chicken." Frank was indeed known for demanding and wanting rapid action, but he was easy-going and endlessly funny at home. He kept me smiling all the time. People knew him as a humble man who listened to and honored others, a man who motivated people to follow him, a man who always sought to learn more, and a man who lived a frugal but value-driven life.

As this remarkable man's widow, I can tell you his success secrets—practices he engaged in that you can replicate. Cultivate all of them, and you'll get further in life than you ever dreamed! Develop even one of these skills, and you'll be ahead of the game.

How did he do it? And much more importantly, what did he do that you can do, too?

You'll find the secrets to his success here. And as you'll see, they're not that hard. But you do need to know them and then act on them.

My challenge for you is: *Try them! Become all you can be!*

LISTEN

Five Ways You Can Develop An Invaluable Skill

Although **Frank was brilliant, as a** schoolboy, he was never more than an average student. No one would have guessed that he'd go on to build a giant global enterprise.

He often admitted to me that he wasn't all that smart. But he would go on to say, **"I have the good fortune to be surrounded by smart people."**

Part of the secret of Frank's success was that he built an excellent talent stack. Of course, finding experts is one thing; keeping them is another. So, how do you surround yourself with intelligent people who stick with you? You listen to them.

Frank knew how to listen.

It takes a certain humility to be a good listener.

Frank had a lot of humility.

When he entered a room for a meeting, he wouldn't just start telling people what to do. Far from a know-it-all, his attitude was, as he'd often tell me, "There's a lot of brain-power in this room, and I want to tap into all of it!"

As he used to say, "None of us is as smart as all of us." He communicated this attitude, not just by saying it, which he frequently did, but also by listening to and valuing what others had to say. You'd be surprised how much this means to people.

Frank Perdue has been gone for many years, yet people still tell me they remember how he would take the time to listen to them and how it made them feel.

"You could talk to him about anything, and he'd listen," George Coffin, from the company's transportation department, told me. "I think he loved the people who worked for him."

The time Frank took to listen showed that he cared, and this approach took him a long way.

If you'd like to raise the bar for your success, practice these skills that I regularly observed in Frank:

1. Listen 90% of the time, talk 10% of the time. I used to watch Frank in both social and business settings. Surprisingly, he didn't talk much. He might start a conversation off with a few questions, but the rest of the time, he'd be carefully listening. He had two goals when listening: he wanted to gather information, but, more importantly, he wanted to let people know that their thoughts and opinions mattered to him.

2. **Give every person your full attention.** If Frank were talking with you, you'd have the sense that, at that moment, you were the most important person in his world. He wasn't thinking about how he would answer you, and he wasn't looking at what else was going on in the room. Instead, his facial expression and body language communicated that you were the focus of his attention, that you were respected and appreciated.

3. **Have body language that doesn't overpower and "use up all the oxygen."** When Frank talked with people, his body language differed from what you might expect from a powerful CEO. You wouldn't see him wielding the large, dominating gestures of a flamboyant, powerful extrovert.

Instead, his small gestures would make you feel like you were talking with a teammate rather than with the "big boss." The result was that you probably felt comfortable talking with him about your ideas.

4. **Listen to your advisors.** Frank was known for being stubborn, but if his advisors could make a good case and convince him they were right, Frank was flexible enough to change his mind. Jack Kelly, the company's governmental affairs advisor, told me, "I never had any problem telling him that the emperor has no clothes. 'You own the business,' I'd tell him, 'and we'll do what you want to do, but you're wrong.'" As Jack told me, Frank would often think it over for an hour or so, change his mind, and go along with Jack's recommendation. And as Frank told me, this approach of listening to experts saved him much grief.

5. **Listen to people whatever their position.** Frank didn't just listen to his trusted advisors. Brian Lipinski, whose specialty at Perdue was packaging, told me, "At the beginning of

my career, I was a peon, but even so, Frank would talk with me very frankly, and I could talk with him the same way. He had no airs about him. It was the same throughout my career. You just talked with him, and he'd sit there and listen." Like thousands of others, Lipinski spent his career with Frank and cherished the relationship. Frank's willingness to listen to Lipinski and others throughout the organization helped create the employee engagement that built a successful company.

Being a good listener paid off for Frank in more ways than one. Hearing from many people at all levels of the organization meant that he made better decisions, but it also gave him the considerable advantage of having employees who stayed with him for their entire careers.

Try it!

HONOR

*Five Ways You Can Gain
Extraordinary Influence*

Having polled companies for decades, Gallup has discovered that organizations in the top quartile for employee engagement outperform those in the bottom quartile with:

- 23% greater profitability
- 43% lower turnover
- 81% lower absenteeism

Frank developed his approach to employee engagement long before this Gallup research became available. However, he had the right instincts. Employee engagement is one of the most critical factors—possibly the most crucial factor—in an organization's success.

What exactly did he do?

Frank was a big believer in the importance of a company's culture. He told me one day, and I wrote it in my diary, **"Values are at the heart of a culture, and part of a leader's job includes creating the culture."**

Frank's cultural values included recognizing people and letting them know that they were valued.

I know of a case when one associate had a newborn with a worrisome high bilirubin level. When my husband heard about it, he tracked down which hospital the baby was in and called the father to ask how his son was doing.

The young father was surprised that the head of his large company would have known about his son. Even more so, he was touched that Frank would take the time to call him. But what amazed him most was that, three hours later, Frank called him back at the hospital.

Frank had sought out one of the world's experts on bilirubin issues and had learned so much about bilirubin that, according to the father, Frank had been able to explain things to him more helpfully than the local doctor had.

On top of this, Frank was ready to make sure that, if needed, the baby would have the best care in the world. The baby recovered rapidly, but the father told me, "You don't forget something like that."

These simple steps Frank took don't cost a penny and can work for you in encouraging a culture of honor, connectedness, and engagement:

1. **Learn people's names.** Frank knew the names of thousands of the people who worked at the plants and the farmers who grew the chickens. Whenever I toured a facility with him, he'd introduce me to workers on the line by name. Not only that, but he'd often tell me something personal about them, such as "Delsie's son just got into college" or "Norton has been with the company for 32 years."

2. **Celebrate with people.** Frank showed his respect by taking the time to attend events that were important to his employees, even when it was outside the workplace. For example, we attended countless weddings.

3. **Be supportive when people face difficulties.** Frank went out of his way to offer comfort, and he did it out of sincere caring. We frequently visited people in the hospital. And when an associate lost a family member, Frank would often drop everything to be among the first to call on the bereaved and condole with them. A person could be four ranks down in the organization and would still hear from Frank.

4. **Attend funerals.** Before knowing Frank, I attended funerals because I believed it was something I was supposed to do. But after watching him, I now realize that it's closer to a sacred privilege, knowing that being there for someone in such a difficult time means so much.

5. **Show retirees that they still matter.** On weekends we would often drive to visit retired people in their homes. Frank still considered former employees "part of the family," even though they no longer received a paycheck. This connection had to be nice for the people we were calling on, but it also sent a message to the current employees that said, "You're important, and I'll still care about you and your service even after you've retired."

The pay-off for having engaged workers or co-workers is that they will often go above and beyond for you. This reward can mean undreamed-of success for you. But engagement is a two-way street. Go above and beyond for them as well.

Try it!

LEAD

Five Ways You Can Garner Undying Loyalty

Getting people to see things your way is one of the most essential ingredients in leadership. When you have this skill, you draw people to your vision in such a way that they'll work hard to make you and your projects a success. People will want to be on your team for life.

Frank Perdue was a master at persuading people to adopt his vision. Excelling at this earned him the support of associates and advisors and enabled him: to become the first chicken operation to build its own feed mill in 1958; its own processing plant in 1968; and its own brand in the 1970s. An astonishing number of people stayed with him their entire careers and were often ready to go the extra mile for him.

The key to how much people want to follow you is how you make them feel about themselves. People want to live up—or live down—to what you think of them. Make people feel valued, trusted, and essential, and they'll tend to want to live up to your view of them.

For example, I've heard people say that when Frank wrote a personal note, they'd keep that note for life. Or when he praised them to their faces, they felt ten feet tall. He was always on the lookout for ways to make people feel important.

Perhaps my favorite example of this was when one employee had worked for many months redesigning the boxes used for shipping fresh chicken from the processing plant to the distributors. The ingenious new configuration allowed more boxes to be loaded per truck, saving fuel and time. Unfortunately, the people on the receiving end didn't like the new boxes, and the design was withdrawn. Frank, understanding the designer's disappointment after a year's work, wanted to make sure the man knew that his work was worthy of recognition. He arranged for a tongue-in-cheek celebration with a genuine bronze plaque, signed by the board of directors, awarding the man "The Great Failed Project Award." The man told me that the humorous "award ceremony" took the sting out of a significant disappointment, and he loved knowing that Frank had his back even when things didn't go well. Though it happened decades ago, the man still talks about it with relish.

This kind of leadership grew a small farm into a company that today has a global footprint.

What are these leadership skills? And how can you use them, whether at work, in your community, or in your family?

1. Make people feel important.

I've already talked about how Frank listened to people and how he honored them. Frank was constantly on the lookout for ways to show his respect and appreciation for the people who worked with him. He even went so far, with my eager participation, as to entertain tens of thousands of Perdue associates for dinner, 100 at a time, in our own home. We did this several times a month for almost seventeen years and ensured that every guest felt valued and recognized. He'd even serve his employees, standing behind the buffet line, waiting on them. How many heads of Fortune 500 size companies would do that?

2. Calibrate your appreciation.

Frank understood what the psychiatrist William James said 100 years ago, "The deepest principle of human nature is the craving for appreciation." Frank acted on this principle, but he took it a step further. Frank understood when an individual craved a big public celebration or when someone might prefer something more private and personal, and he calibrated the recognition to what fit the individual.

3. **Encourage others to have ownership.** When Frank wanted a problem solved, he wasn't into micromanaging the solution. His default approach was to explore the problem with the team in charge of solving it. He would tell them the results he was looking for, but he encouraged them to figure out innovative ways to get there. They owned the project, including the solution and its implementation. By following this approach, Frank made his employees feel necessary, capable, and, most of all, engaged.

4. **Cherish people who stand up to you.** Frank gave people the respect of welcoming their opinions, even

when they were negative. People who
did well in the company were almost
always standing up to Frank and telling
him what he needed to hear. He showed
them that he valued their points of
view, even when (or maybe I should say,
primarily when) those views strongly
differed from his own. His willingness to
consider other points of view increased
people's sense of engagement. They
knew their perspectives mattered. And
by the way, the man who argued with
Frank most vociferously, Don Mabe,
even told him one day, "You should
retire and take up hang gliding." Mabe
was the man Frank later chose to become president of his company.

5. **Be egalitarian.** I've watched Frank
   with the President of the United States
   and with factory workers on the line,
   and he treated them all with equal
   respect. When walking on the line, I
   noticed that he never had the attitude
   of, "I'm the boss." Instead, it was,
   "We're all a team, and while I have
   my role, I very much respect and value
   your role." He made people feel like
   part of his team.

Developing this kind of inspirational approach to leadership is a soft skill, but you can learn it. It can help you in all your relationships.

Try it!

NETWORK

*Five Ways You Can Connect
with People for Maximum
Impact*

Some might say that Frank Perdue exuded charisma. However, Frank wasn't naturally gregarious. Growing up on a farm, he rarely had opportunities to socialize. People back then characterized him as introverted. In fact, to the end of his days, he was a shy man. But, to me, his social skills and his understanding of human nature seemed to be boundless. For example, I used to watch in awe how good he was at networking.

Imagine for a moment that you were to accompany Frank to a United Way function. (This, by the way, was a charity he adored.) For starters, if the event were to begin at 6:00 pm, the two of you would be there two minutes early, at 5:58 pm.

Inside the room, you would notice that Frank would position himself about 30 feet from the door to have a chance to interact with each person as they entered the room.

Typically, each contact would be brief,

but, in observing Frank, you would notice that as he greeted someone, he would look each individual in the eyes while shaking their hand. He would focus his attention to envelop the person in his caring so totally that the individual was almost certain to feel at that moment like the most important person in Frank's world. In truth, at that moment, that person *was* the most important person in Frank's world.

Frank had planned it by positioning himself near the entrance and making an effort to talk with each of the people attending the event. A couple of hours later, you and he would have shaken hands with everyone in the room at the end of the event. And you would be in the unique position to know that this didn't happen by accident.

Frank was so insightful to engage a room in this way.

Business leaders often go to charity and other events to network and to be seen supporting a cause. However, after they've invested the time and the money to be there, how many of them genuinely accomplish their networking and visibility goals as thoughtfully and efficiently as Frank did?

Frank's social skills at events were always

a bravura performance—although on thinking it over, maybe I shouldn't use the word "performance." His efforts came from the heart, so it wasn't about performing. His actions showed who he indeed was.

His impressive social skills weren't limited to significant social events. I often meet people even today who remember a brief contact with Frank: an administrative assistant in an office where Frank was visiting and took the time to make her feel important; a taxi driver who for the rest of his life remembered the pleasure of having Frank talk with him about the cab driver's work, family and life; or a server at a restaurant who remembered Frank treating him with the dignity of an equal.

Frank benefited greatly from knowing lots of people, and so will you. You want to be top of mind when a person is, for example, considering hiring or appointing you to a position, buying your product, or even inviting you to a great party.

Follow Frank's ways for networking a room:

1. **Be intentional.** Remind yourself before every event why you're attending. If your goal is the general visibility that supports "brand you," pay atten-

tion to your clothes, body language, and posture. Are there particular people you need or want to meet? List them. Then pay special attention to each person with whom you interact. Are you looking for sales possibilities? List them too. Are there people from whom you'd like to learn? Whatever your purpose in being there, be intentional about achieving it.

2. **Arrive early.** Entering a room even a minute or two before others will enable you to talk with people before the room becomes crowded. After all, you've probably paid to be at this event, so maximize your investment in time and money.

3. **Stand reasonably close to the entrance.** Depending on the size of the hall, it could be a couple of car lengths, more or less. That way, you can meet the maximum number of people as they come in.

4. **Interact with as many people as you can.** If the group is up to 100 people, try to interact with all of them. I bet this won't come naturally, but it can be done. I saw Frank do it all the time.

5. Make notes about follow-up.

Frank was known for writing notes about contacts or opportunities and keeping the notes in his shirt pocket until he had followed up on them. Whether you're exchanging business cards or doing it through a smartphone, make a note for each person about what the follow-up should be. Maybe you will send them a book. Maybe you will introduce them to someone. Maybe you'd like to take them to lunch. Maybe you'd like to put them on your mailing list. Whatever it is, make a note of it. The reason? Unless your memory is exceptional (and far better than mine), when you're at your hotel that night looking at many dozens of cards or names, you may not remember. Then you've lost an opportunity for which you paid good money.

Networking is a vital skill. You've heard the old cliché, "It's not what you know; it's who you know." Well, it got to be a cliché because it's so true.

Actually, don't forget about the "what

you know" part of the saying because of course, that's vital also, and I will talk about that next. As I often say, "One good idea can change your life," but it's also true that one good contact can change your life. Or as Frank used to say, "You never know which key turns the lock."

Grow your networking skills!

Try it!

LEARN

Five Ways You Can Become an
Insatiable "Informavore"

You probably don't know the word "informavore." Or, then again, maybe you do.

I thought I had made up the word, but when I googled it, I discovered that indeed it is a word. Not only is "informavore" a word, but it means exactly what I intended: someone who consumes information.

As I mentioned earlier, "One good idea can change your life." Oh, and it can also put you way ahead of your competitors.

Frank loved to quote the story of an old sea captain who told his son, "My competition copies everything I do, but they can't copy my mind, and I leave 'em huffing and puffing a mile and a half behind." For Frank, the agility that resulted from research and the ability to put ideas into action were the magic keys to leaving competitors "huffing and puffing a mile and a half behind."

A lot of Frank's success began with getting the good ideas. He put enormous effort into this. Here's one example. It has to do with building a feed mill complex for producing chicken feed.

Building a feed mill is a surprisingly complex job. Here's how Frank went about it.

Before beginning construction, he began researching what it would take to build the grain tanks. This, by the way, was something characteristic of Frank throughout his career: When he was starting something new, he put into action his favorite Alexander Hamilton quote, "When I have a subject in hand, I study it profoundly. Day and night, it is before me. My mind becomes pervaded with it."

In the case of the feed mill, he started his research by calling an engineer at one of the feed companies, Purina, to ask what kind of steel to use in constructing the tank. "This was somewhat brazen of me," Frank said, "given that I was a competitor, but he told me exactly what I needed to know."

Frank needed this information because when you fill a grain storage tank with a quarter of a million bushels of corn in 100-degree summer weather, and then the tank and its contents contract in zero-degree weather in winter, the steel seams can split. The result is grain spilled all over the ground, meaning both waste and expense.

Poorly constructed grain storage tanks were causing a lot of these kinds of problems back then, and Frank didn't want this to happen in his feed mill complex. Fortunately, the Purina engineer shared his expertise on the kind of high-quality, flexible steel needed to avoid the issue.

That was only the beginning of Frank's research. He contacted countless people asking countless questions. Harold Shockley, one of the people who worked on this project, told me, "I toured several plants in other states, and when I'd tell people there whom I worked for, they'd say, 'Frank Perdue? That SOB! He must have called me with 150 questions!'"

As Shockley went on to say, "There wasn't a plant that I ever visited where they didn't know who Frank was because he had called each of them at least several times. He called every soybean plant in the country, and he'd ask them every question you can think of, even including 'How much money did you make per bushel last year?'"

Since this was proprietary information, the usual response to Frank was, "None of your business." But that didn't keep Frank from continuing to try, and every once in a while, it would pay off.

Frank felt that getting helpful information was worth just about any price in terms of time and effort throughout his life. In this case, he was amazed by how much proprietary information he could get just by asking.

Frank gave as well as got. When he'd visit a competitor's grain facilities, or for that matter, any other facilities that interested him, he'd always offer to reciprocate and have them tour his operation. It surprised him that only about four ever took him up on his offer out of the hundreds of people he saw over the years.

This kind of research characterized Frank throughout his career. He put the same effort into researching how to build a processing plant. He once spent weeks talking to butchers in New York City about what they were looking for in chicken. He did the same with advertising agencies when he wanted to brand his chicken, which had never been done before.

Frank would dive into it if it interested him, even when a subject had nothing to do with business. He was passionately interested, as far as I could tell, in just about everything.

He was always reading, and the topics that interested him were diverse. He knew enough about Empress Catherine the Great to have a lively discussion about her with the Librarian of Congress. He read about the construction of the Brooklyn Bridge. You wouldn't believe how much he knew about the racehorse Seabiscuit, treasure hunting, military history, or the latest John Grisham novel, which he loved to discuss with his friend, a local judge.

When a subject interested him, he'd do a deep dive, studying about it. I remember he knew so much about Alexander Hamilton that something unique happened when we visited the Hamilton Museum on Nevis Island, where Hamilton was born.

After maybe ten minutes of showing us around, the docent pointed to an object and said she wasn't sure what it was. Frank knew and could explain where it came from and what its function was.

After that, things on the tour changed. The three of us continued walking through the museum, but now as we looked at the artifacts and posters, the docent asked Frank about the objects we were looking at. They had reversed roles.

It was as if she were a student and Frank a professor. That's how much Frank knew about Alexander Hamilton! And further, he pretty much knew about any of the artifacts and in tremendous detail.

Frank was a true "informavore." He drew inspiration from reading, attending lectures, hanging out with other people in business, and generally putting himself in the way of getting good ideas.

And what about you? Keep doing all the things you'd be doing anyway, like listening to podcasts, haunting the Internet, setting up Google alerts for topics you care about, but in addition:

1. **Read everything you can.** It doesn't have to be disciplined reading. It's better if it isn't because often good ideas come from where you least expect them.

2. **Attend conventions and other social events.** I've gotten to know several convention organizers, and I guarantee they put unbelievable effort into getting great speakers who can give you the best, most current ideas and information. In addition to conventions, attend social events to use your networking skills to meet new people with new ideas.

3. **Join professional associations
   in your field.** You'll be hanging
   out with people who spend their lives
   thinking about the same issues you are.

4. **Sign up for newsletters.** Even if
   you don't learn anything from a particular newsletter, it might spark your
   mind with a new idea.

5. **Join a mastermind group or hire
   a coach.** Some of us, myself included, thought that we could come up
   with all the needed inspiration and
   knowledge on our own. But it's not
   true. A wise mastermind group or an
   intelligent coach can give you ideas
   that are right for you and that it might
   take you ten years to discover on your
   own.

To be innovative, be an "Informavore." Do
what it takes to find good ideas. The reason?
"One good idea can change your life." And
lots of good ideas can lead to undreamed of
success. An intense drive to find the best ideas
characterized Frank Perdue's entire life.
   Try it!

SAVE

Five Ways You Can Acquire What Really Matters

Frank Perdue was a big believer in the David Copperfield Secret of Happiness.

By the way, we're not talking about my favorite magician; we're talking about the novel by Charles Dickens. A character in *David Copperfield*, Mr. Micawber advised: Spend *less* than your income, and you'll be happy. Spend *more*, and you'll be miserable.

Frank was a big believer in living way, way below your means. For him, the money he didn't spend meant there was money available to take advantage of opportunities that came his way. It meant the chance to invest or to be philanthropic.

I don't think I ever saw him spend money for the sake of ego. He got his identity through creating or serving, not through spending.

Frank Perdue lived the Copperfield happiness secret because he was a frugal man to the core. He always lived astonishingly below his income. Our home, for example, was a comfortable ranch house with neighbors that included retired teachers and a guy who ran a grain elevator. Trust me, millionaire's row it was not.

I have a favorite memory of this. One day in the late 1990s, Owen Schweers, the Perdue Director of Packaging, was to bring an important business person to meet Frank at our Salisbury home. As Schweers pulled up beside our house, his VIP passenger started laughing heartily.

"Okay, that's a good one!" he chortled. "But you're not going to get me on this. I *know* Frank Perdue wouldn't live in that little ranch house!"

Schweers stopped his car near our front door. "No," Schweers insisted, "this is Frank's house."

"*Sure, right,*" said the VIP, still guffawing.

Suddenly, his laughter stopped because Frank opened the door and then stepped outside to greet his guests. "Wow," whispered the VIP to Schweers, "Frank really does live here!"

Living in a modest house was typical of Frank. The fact is, most status symbols left him cold.

For example, when we traveled, which

we did while visiting overseas buyers, we could have used a chauffeur-driven limousine. Instead, Frank made it a point to use the local subways.

This use of everyday travel happened whether it was New York, London, Moscow, Tokyo, or Beijing. His ego didn't require a limousine.

Once in 1993, we spent six weeks driving from Maryland to California and back. Where did he, the head of Perdue Farms, and I, a Sheraton heiress, stay? Motel 6, every night. We did it because this chain was clean, always friendly, and the check-in procedures were wonderfully rapid.

Frank continuously encouraged his kids in this kind of thinking. As he told his children in one of the family newsletters in which he was encouraging them to live below their means: "It's not fun to be worried about whether you can pay your bills."

Frank was frugal, and the money he didn't spend went to philanthropy for the most part. He felt a more profound and lasting pleasure supporting, for instance, United Way than spending money on himself.

Could avoiding status-type spending add to your happiness? Would the David

Copperfield approach be right for you? How can you be super-intentional about what you spend money on while adding value to your life?

Here is a Billionaire's Approach to Being Frugal:

1. **Live in a less expensive house than you can afford.** Way less.

2. **Buy quality clothes but make them last.** Re-weavers for repairs can be a good investment when you have quality clothes. If you haven't ever used a re-weaver, you may find their results astonishing. When Alice Zotta had finished re-weaving a worn-through elbow or knee, I couldn't detect where she had done it. It was the equivalent of a brand new jacket or pair of trousers. Similarly, make your cobbler your best friend! I promise you, Frank did. In our 17 years of marriage before his passing, Frank bought only three pairs of shoes. I suspect we had the highest cobbler bill in Maryland because I was forever getting his shoes resoled.

4. **Make your car last.** Frank took great care of his car, and he drove the same car during our entire 17 years.

5. **Fly economy.** Even if you can afford to fly first class, go economy. Frank said, "You get there just as fast, so why pay more?" He certainly could have afforded to fly first class, but his ego didn't require it. His attitude was that unless there's a medical reason or a person is very tall, going first class is a waste.

6. **Use public transportation.** When you travel on business or vacation, use public transportation like buses and subways. Frank knew the New York subway system better than most New Yorkers, and when we traveled abroad, which we often did because he'd call on the primary buyers of Perdue chicken in other countries, we'd always use the local subways. He wanted to get a better feel for a city by using the same transportation everyone else did. He also liked using public transportation because it's ecological. And on buses, you'll meet people and hear stories you might never hear otherwise.

There are many advantages to being frugal. Most of all, as Frank told me and also told his children, having savings available means the ability to take advantage of opportunities, whether investments or philanthropy. It emphasizes being a good steward, as opposed to having an identity that depends on status symbols.

Try it!

LEAVE A LEGACY

Five Ways You Can Ensure Your Values Outlive You

Frank Perdue received many nota-ble awards over the years, such as the Golden Plate from the American Academy of Achievement in 1983 and the Edison Achievement Award in 1991. Frank kept them in his closet. He wouldn't have gone along with hanging them anywhere more public because accolades were not his priority.

As much as I admired Frank for his business success, I admired him even more for his success as a family man. He put tremendous thought and effort into his family life. One of the most meaningful and moving things he did for his family was that he didn't just leave them material things but also his "ethical will."

Both of us had observed that wealth without values leads to unhappiness. Frank and his first wife, Madeline, instilled good values in their children from birth; however, we knew that an inheritance could sometimes short-circuit this process. There was a phrase we both related to: "Adversity breeds character. Prosperity breeds monsters." Lack of values can make children vulnerable to destructive behaviors, it can turn heirs into playboys, and it can accelerate the arc of "shirtsleeves to shirtsleeves in three generations."

You've probably noted yourself that wealth without values can lead to unhappiness. It can make children more vulnerable to destructive behaviors such as substance abuse or getting their identity by irresponsible spending.

By the time he was in his 80s, Frank had come to believe that people with integrity, that is, people who follow their highest values, will lead happier lives. These people gain self-respect and the trust of others, so they have successful relationships not just with others but with themselves. Frank was ready to embrace the idea of embedding these values in his family culture so they would still exist after his passing.

Ethical wills are not something new, by the way; they've existed since Biblical times. I suggested that Frank use this ancient practice to help make sure his ideas were codified and passed down to future generations. We both felt that by putting these ideas in writing, especially knowing that his children would read these ideas during his funeral, an ethical will would impact the family culture.

"What is an ethical will?" you ask. Maybe the best way to explain it is by showing what it does.

If you decide to create your own ethical will, it can clarify your values. If you have children, it can help them, and those after them live happy, productive lives. An ethical will can accomplish this by writing the values you believe will be good guides for behaving during our time on this planet.

Ideally, your ethical will can become part of your family's culture. When your children and their children are looking for meaning and identity, it reminds them, "This is the kind of people we are."

He and I spent three full days on the project. Frank didn't type so that he would dictate his ideas; I'd type them, we'd discuss them, and then I'd type his changes. By the end of the process, there wasn't a single word that Frank hadn't put his heart into. He gave it the seriousness it deserved.

At his funeral, each grandchild read one of the parts of his ethical will. Since then, every family member, including new members through marriage, received a framed copy of it. Many of them tell me they keep it on their desks.

Here's **Frank's Ethical Will**:

1. Be honest always.
2. Be a person whom others are justified in trusting.
3. If you say you will do something, do it.
4. You don't have to be the best, but you should be the best you can be.
5. Treat all people with courtesy and respect, no exceptions.
6. Remember that the way to be happy is to think of what you can do for others. The way to be miserable is to think about what people should be doing for you.
7. Be part of something bigger than yourself. That something can be family, the pursuit of knowledge, the environment, or whatever you choose.
8. Remember that hard work is satisfying and fulfilling.
9. Nurture the ability to laugh and have fun.
10. Have respect for those who have gone before, learn from their weaknesses, and build on their strengths.

If you want to create an ethical will, here are the steps Frank and I took:

1. **Analyze the values that work in your family.**
2. **Make a list of all of these values.** Brainstorm as many as you can. You may find that the ones that weren't the immediately obvious ones turn out to be the most valuable.
3. **Cut your list down to ten or fewer.** Frank and I originally came up with 50 values that we cared about. However, Frank understood that a more extended list risks losing impact.
4. **Get feedback from family members.** Then revise and finalize it.
5. **Plan how you'll use it.** Will it be read at your funeral? Do you want family members to know it now? Do you want copies engraved on a copper plate, which is given to each family member, signaling the document's importance? Would you like to have it read at family holidays and family reunions?

Letting family members know your values can provide them with guidelines for their lives. It can help them at the end of their days to feel, "My life was worthwhile. I led a good life."

Try it!

MY GIFT TO YOU

Wrapping It All Up in a Bow

I've often thought the greatest gift one person can give another is inspiration. The thing about inspiration is that it provides you with direction and energy. What it does (and I'm feeling presumptuous saying this, but I'm going to say it regardless): **Inspiration gives people a better vision of themselves.**

Full disclosure, I'm 80 years old and still working on this and having a blast doing it! No matter where you are in life, starting out, in the middle of your career, or looking back on your life, you can always get closer to being the best you can be.

But back to Frank Perdue. He told me that as a child, he had no visions of being a successful businessman. He wasn't predestined for success. And yet, the company he built has defied the odds and is still going strong more than 100 years later.

As a future titan of industry, known

worldwide for his marketing success, Frank started with no experience beyond working in a father-and-son chicken business. He didn't have any of the social connections he might have had if he had lived in a city, connections that might have been a shortcut to success.

However, Frank was able to transcend every obstacle. He grew not just broadly in the skill sets he acquired but also vertically: that is, he rose from a shy, introverted young man to someone comfortable on the world stage.

As you read this list, ask yourself if you can master the skills that he did. Um….er, before you answer, here's a hint from me: *If Frank Perdue did it, you can! I know you can! YOU CAN!*

Here's how he did it.

- Frank developed unusually effective listening skills.
- He honed the skills needed for making others feel important.
- He made himself into a leader whom others wanted to follow.
- He mastered the art of networking.
- He was constantly on the lookout for good ideas.
- His frugality enabled him to have the cash to grow his business.
- He led a values-driven life.

Frank became more than he was born with. He did hundreds of small things that expanded his skill set, human relations skills, and ability to think big.

The steps needed to do all these are small—the rewards for doing them, tremendous.

Try them! Become all you can be!

FRANK SAID

The Quotable Frank Perdue

Frank Perdue was an introverted man who learned, through study and hard work, how to express himself succinctly and purposefully. Over the years, and I think it would amaze him if he were alive today, people remembered what he said and quote him rather often. Here are a few gems from a man who thought it could be done, so he went and did it.

In your 20s, you learn.
In your 30s, you earn.

A business that doesn't change is a business that is going to die.

If you believe in unlimited quality and act in all your business dealings with total integrity, the rest will take care of itself.

*If you can differentiate a dead chicken,
you can differentiate anything.*

*Find out what the customer wants and
then make it better.*

*If the quality is there, the consumer will
want it, buy it and pay for it.*

*Market share is king. You cannot afford
to replace lost market share.*

*Quality is the one absolutely necessary
ingredient of all the most successful
companies in the world.*

*No one ever complained their way
to the top.*

*I can't tell by looking in your eyes
whether you're a priest or a crook.*

ABOUT THE
AUTHOR

Mitzi Perdue

How many others who write on the business greats got to see them up close and personal the way Mitzi Perdue got to see her husband, Frank Perdue? The fresh approach you can see in this, her latest book, comes in part because she's a professional writer. Still, on top of that, she also has a master's degree in administration and could look at Frank's actions from an academic point of view and a practical this-is-the-real world approach.

"I'm eager to share Frank's wisdom," Mitzi says. "My wish for everyone is that they get to be all they can be. Learning from Frank is a shortcut to fulfillment and success."

Mitzi's background includes being the daughter of the Co-Founder and President of the Sheraton Hotels, Ernest Henderson, a Harvard BA with honors in Government, and a syndicated columnist for Scripps Howard. Her column, the Environment and You,

was the most widely syndicated environmental column in the US for years. Currently, she writes for *Psychology Today*, *Wealth Management*, and the Association of Foreign Press Correspondents. She also hosts the EarthX TV series, *The Pen and the Planet*.

Mitzi Perdue
www.MitziPerdue.com
+1 (410) 860-4444 (Office)

READ MORE

These excellent titles from our Life-Changing Classics Series are available at TremendousLeadership.com